NEW ENGLAND

MALLARD
PRESS

Photography
FPG
Odyssey Publishing Ltd

Photo Editor
Annette Lerner

MALLARD PRESS

An imprint of BDD Promotional
Book Company Inc.,
666 Fifth Avenue, New York,
NY 10103

Mallard Press and its
accompanying design and logo
are trademarks of BDD
Promotional Book Company, Inc.

Color separation by Advance
Laser Graphic Arts, Hong Kong.

Printed and bound
in Hong Kong.

ISBN 0-7924-5487-7

*Previous pages: bare rock near
Pemaquid Lighthouse, and (right)
white water in the Mattawamkeag
Wilderness Area, both in Maine.*

Nearly thirteen million people live in the six New England states, and each thinks their surroundings are typical of New England, which gives rise to differences of opinion. Is New England best represented by the steeple of Boston's Old North Church, the mountains of New Hampshire, or the sand dunes of Cape Cod?

Even within individual states the differences are striking. A Maine lobsterman wouldn't trade his awe-inspiring seaside cliffs and the roar of the surf for a potato farm in northern Maine, and neither of them will ever be convinced that the wooded hills of Vermont are nearly as romantic as their own forests. Vermont farmers would never dream of trading their green valleys for such an obviously infertile place as Cape Cod, no matter how beautiful the Cape may be. Cape Codders often run down to Rhode Island, but often just to see if it's true that they put tomatoes in their clam chowder. And along Narraganset Bay, people find it hard to believe that anyone could really enjoy life in a place like Connecticut, where the summer sun gets hot enough to grow tobacco. Of course, people who do enjoy life in Connecticut can't imagine living in the Berkshires, where most people haven't the foggiest notion how to handle a sailboat.

New England is as much tied to the sea as to the mountains, to its sophisticated cities as much as quiet country towns – it is as industrial as it is agricultural. But wherever you go, from Nantucket up to Presque Isle; from the Saint John River down to Candlewood Lake; from Cape Ann to Lake Champlain, there isn't anything about New England that isn't beautiful. And it's at its very best in the fall.

Fall begins up in northern Maine about the middle of September. It spreads south quickly and, most years, all New England is doused with brilliant color by mid-October. The chemistry that lights up the forest and touches something wonderful in the human spirit has to do with the tightening of cells in the structure of leaves, cutting off the production of chlorophyll and turning them wonderfully from green to red, yellow, scarlet and hundreds of other colors. The work is done at night when the temperature drops below forty-five degrees, to be admired during the crisp, sunny days when nothing in the world is better than just being alive.

The maple, a tree that thrives in all its varieties all over New England, is the star of the show. It is the world's most colorful tree and the only one that turns different colors: some red, some yellow, all indescribably beautiful. Poplars and birches turn lemon yellow; dogwood, mountain ash and barberry become rich red. Those brownish-red trees are probably beeches, and the rich browns are most likely oaks. They put on their finery against a backdrop of rich green pine and hemlock, and together add up to what New Englander P.T. Barnum once called "the second-greatest show on earth."

Sadly, it has a limited run. Though everyone wishes it could go on forever, the fall-foliage season is only two or three weeks long. It lures thousands of what the natives call "leaf-peepers," to the region and, in spite of the term, New Englanders enhance the experience with a hearty welcome, making it a time for country fairs, auctions and roadside-farm stands banked up with pumpkins and juicy apples, jugs of maple syrup and jars of homemade preserves. It's the time for church suppers and bazaars, arts festivals, house tours and historic reenactments; in fact, just about anything that will encourage the leaf-peepers to stay a little longer and sample New England hospitality.

The leaves usually lure people to the mountains, but the New England autumn also makes the coast a perfect October destination. Fall color enlivens the trees there too, and the sea is more dramatic for the change of season. The sun is still warm and the water is warm enough to take the chill off the onshore breeze. Best of all, there is that wonderful feeling of solitude that can be so dramatically sensed on a beach after summer has gone and winter is still off in the distance.

At that stage, winter is too far off for many New Englanders. Some of them think winter is the best of all times there when the mountains are covered with snow and the ski slopes are calling to them. They may be right. It all depends on where you find pleasure. One thing is certain, whatever your pleasure, you'll find it in New England.

Left: the 1858 Bass Harbor Head Light overlooks a still sea on the southern tip of Mount Desert Island, Maine. Its craggy perch has made this light a favorite subject with artists and photographers, especially at sunset. Numerous such lights are a feature of the treacherous Maine coastline, where severe Atlantic storms regularly pound the famous granite cliffs of the state. The southeast shoreline (below) of Mount Desert Island falls under the protection of Acadia National Park, the great attraction of this part of Maine. The park was established in 1919.

Facing page top: the smooth, reflective waters of Jordan Pond, situated at the foot of the cliffs of Penobscot Mountain in Acadia National Park, Maine. One of the park's most beautiful sites, this stretch of water is popular with fishermen as its well-oxygenated waters provide the perfect habitat for trout and salmon. Facing page bottom: the dainty white footbridge that leads to Mount Desert Island Museum, Maine. Right: fishing floats cast aside at Owl's Head, a resort village south of Rockport in Penobscot Bay, Maine.

Above: cruisers in Friendship
Harbor, Maine. This coastal village
is best known for the Friendship
sloop, which originated here. A
small, sturdy, all-purpose craft, the
sloop was first built in the early
twentieth century. Now it is usually
only used for pleasure, but once it
was the most popular boat of its
day. Right: Boothbay Harbor,
formerly a simple fishing village
but now known as the boating
capital of New England. For three
days in July, Boothbay Harbor
hosts Windjammer Days, a
boating celebration involving
parades, pageants and community
suppers. Thousands of visitors are
attracted every summer, and most
of them are keen to see the
authentic Windjammer Fleet of
sailing vessels. These arrive for
the event from their home port of
Camden Harbor (facing page),
Maine.

Left: still water in the early morning at Bucksport, Maine. Bucksport lies on the east bank of the Penobscot River, its main street running parallel with the waterway. Right: the Stars and Stripes flies proudly over Quoddy Head Lighthouse. A lighthouse has stood on Quoddy Head – the easternmost point of America – since 1807, looking out from Maine across the Bay of Fundy towards Canada.

Echo Lake reflects the mountain pass of Franconia Notch in perfectly still water on a calm day in the fall. Set in the White Mountains, scenic Franconia Notch is one of New Hampshire's most popular tourist destinations, especially in the fall.

Above: a railroad car of the Conway Scenic Railroad being pulled along by a steam locomotive in the White Mountains of New Hampshire (these pages). The railroad operates from the North Conway Depot, taking passengers on an eleven-mile trip around Mount Washington Valley. Built in 1874, the station saw regular passenger-train service until 1961. Its quaint Victorian layout remains intact. Left: the Flume, a narrow gorge that boasts a beautiful waterfall at Franconia Notch. It was discovered by a ninety-three-year-old woman who found it while on a somewhat adventurous fishing trip! Facing page: Lower Falls Scenic Area on the Swift River.

In contrast to the bright blaze of fall color, the monochrome tones of a Vermont winter landscape (left) are stark and severe, but nevertheless, the countryside is not deserted at this time – now is when the skiers arrive. Most famous for the fabulous skiing (below) provided by a series of trails and downhill runs on the interconnected slopes of Mount Mansfield and Spruce Peak, Stowe, in Vermont, has developed into a sophisticated year-round resort. Mount Mansfield, Vermont's highest mountain, provides a challenge for the most expert skier.

Facing page: the village church reflects the colors of fall in East Orange, Vermont, and (right) a Hereford cow grazes on the last grass of summer as the tone of the trees heralds the approach of winter near Lake Willoughby, northern Vermont. Below: the gold-leafed dome of the State Capitol of Vermont in Montpelier, the smallest state capital in the nation. Montpelier, a town of some 9,000 souls, has been the seat of Vermont's government since 1805. The Capitol, constructed of Vermont granite, was built in 1857 and crowned with a statue of Ceres, the Roman goddess of agriculture, as a mark of the importance of that industry to Vermont. The Capitol interior is richly decorated, indeed, the Senate Chamber is considered to be the finest room in the state.

The Charles River Basin, Beacon Hill and the downtown skyline in Boston, the world-renowned capital of Massachusetts, known as the "Athens of America."

Above: the grand, Renaissance-style First Church of Christ, Scientist – the mother church of the Christian Science Church in Boston. It was built of Indiana limestone in 1894 and is now a Boston landmark, as well known as the Massachusetts State House (right). The latter's gold-leaf dome was added in 1874, replacing the copper sheets supplied by Paul Revere. He and Samuel Adams, another revolutionary, laid the building's cornerstone in 1795. Facing page: the Custom House tower from Marine Park. The twenty-nine-story, 495-foot tower was added to the huge edifice in 1915, making it the tallest building in New England at that time.

Facing page: Beaver II, *part of the Boston Tea Party Ship and Museum at Griffin Wharf, Boston. From here on December 16,1773, three clippers loaded with chests of tea were relieved of their cargo, which was tipped into Boston Harbor in protest against the nominal tax on tea. The slow build-up to the American Revolution had begun. Right: Rockport Harbor on Cape Ann, Massachusetts. Rockport has been an artists' colony since the twenties and, as such, is a mecca for tourists who flock to the art galleries of its Main Street.*

Facing page: a grist mill from the 1600s, similar to the sort the Puritans would once have used, at Plymouth, Massachusetts. Site of the first permanent colony in New England, Plymouth is still a place of pilgrimage for Americans. The Plymouth Rock Memorial (below) encases the boulder traditionally accepted as the Pilgrims' stepping stone from their ship in the dead of winter in1620. It was designed by McKim, Mead and White and has become one of the most famous landmarks in the world. Right: a beached sailboat on Nauset Marsh, Cape Cod. Beaches in this part of Massachusetts are among the finest in the world.

Left: the First Congregational Church in Yarmouth Port, Cape Cod, Massachusetts. Yarmouth was the third town on the Cape, founded on the South Shore in 1639. Walking tours of the Botanic Trails of Yarmouth cover fifty-three acres of preserved lands, beginning in the center of the town. Above and facing page: Provincetown on Cape Cod, Massachusetts. This was the place where the Pilgrims first landed, albeit very briefly; they were later to set sail again for Plymouth as Provincetown was thought to be unsuitable as a spot for settlement. Today the town is home to a collection of fishermen, artists and writers, who evidently disagree with the Pilgrims' view.

Below: Herring Cove beach, Provincetown. Tucked into the northern tip of Cape Cod, Provincetown is perfectly situated as a base from which to explore the miles of glorious beaches that make up the Cape Cod National Seashore. The town attracts about twelve times its indigenous population during the vacation season of July and August and is largely devoted to catering for these visitors. Despite the numbers, it is still possible to find solitude among the rolling dunes and vast beaches.
Right: fishing boats and pleasure craft casually moored on Martha's Vineyard, an island comprising small fishing villages and summer resorts, rolling heathland, lakes and forests, as well as colorful cliffs and fine beaches.

Facing page: Edgartown Harbor Light on Martha's Vineyard, Massachusetts. A light was established here in 1928 on an island connected to the mainland by a little bridge, a favorite trysting place for the locals. The hurricane of 1938 destroyed both light and bridge, so the Coastguard thought to replace them with a steel tower. However, the locals petitioned against this and the authorities answered their pleas by using another nineteenth-century light brought from Ipswich, Massachusetts, in 1939. Above: a delicate shell-pink sunset over the Nashaquitsa Cliffs at Gay Head, on the most westerly point of Martha's Vineyard, and (left) a fine day at Ocean Park in Oak Bluffs on the east coast of the island. Oak Bluffs is famed for its ornate Victorian architecture.

Facing page: Block Island in the snow. Located ten miles south of Rhode Island, this wild and beautiful retreat was named for a Dutch navigator who explored the region in 1614. Right: Newport, where, around the turn of the century, millionaires started to build their versions of summer "cottages" along the shore. Inspired by the great palaces of Europe, these residences dripped money and self-importance. Today many are open to the public.

These pages: Rhode Island.
Above right: Point Judith Light,
which lies at the point where the
waters of Narragansett Bay and
Long Island Sound meet. The first
wooden tower was established in
1810. It was demolished by a
hurricane in 1815 and was
replaced the following year by the
present thirty-five-foot-high stone
tower. In 1938 an even greater
hurricane destroyed the larger part
of the lighthouse's seawall and
thirty feet of the beach in front of it,
but the tower withstood the storm.
There is also a coastguard station
on this site. Right: high masts of
fine yachts in Newport Harbor for
the Regatta. The ultra-wealthy of
this town were responsible for the
development of yacht racing in the
area before the First World War,
and this ultimately led to the
establishment of that great
transatlantic yacht race, the
America's Cup.

Distinctive beside the city's office blocks and skyscrapers, Connecticut's State Capitol in Hartford stands resplendent, an unusual combination of Gothic Revivalism topped by a gold-encased, Classical dome.

Facing page and right: Yale University in Connecticut. Named for Elihu Yale, its wealthy merchant benefactor, Yale University is one of the most distinguished in the United States. It is also one of the oldest, founded in 1701 by a group of Puritan clergymen in Clinton and moved to its present site in New Haven in 1716. It has since grown to enrol over 10,000 students a year. Gothic Revival buildings dominate the Yale campus, their walls clad in creepers that underline the university's Ivy League status. Southport Harbor (below), southwest of Fairfield, was part of a wealthy shipping center in the nineteenth century and as such, its historic district can now boast nearly 200 fine eighteenth- and nineteenth-century houses.

Two fully rigged, original sailing vessels are the main attractions in the Mystic Seaport Museum (these pages) at the mouth of the Mystic River in Connecticut. One is the Charles W. Morgan (right), the last survivor of America's nineteenth-century whaling fleet. Here only the cars and the clothes of visitors give away the fact that this is a reconstructed nineteenth-century port, rather than some forgotten backwater that chose not to modernize. The museum is justifiably the best known feature of Mystic, a village which has been building ships since the seventeenth century. Overleaf: a New England fall.